Copyright © (2020) by Karen Boddie

ISBN – 978-1-7348081-3-1

Library of Congress Control Number 2020907880

And Then You Go Shopping

Written by: Karen Boddie

Publishing by: Exposed Books Publishing

Text Formation by: Exposed Books Publishing and Karen Boddie

Printed in the United States of America

Website: www.authorkarenb.com

Acknowledgement

So many persons have contributed to the birth of this book.

First and foremost, I thank God for trusting me with and giving me the vision from which to birth this project.

Thank you to my friends and family who have supported me throughout "And Then You Go Shopping." Some of you have been there with me since the initial vision. Others came on this journey a little later. Each of you know what part you played. Thank you to those who: provided words of encouragement, read from those initial notes when I was still contemplating if I really needed to write this book, did check-ins with me to see where I was in terms of progress, kept me on track, and most of all, pushed me through. Although I dare not start naming everyone, I will acknowledge a few extra special persons.

To my mother Juanita Backers - who is my biggest supporter and number one fan-You are THE definition of a true survivor.

To Brandon and Justin, two of my strongest supporters - I am so grateful to God for blessing me with both of you. I learn something from you each and every day. Thank you for your encouraging words throughout this process. You have poured and continue to pour support into me that you don't even realize.

To my sisters Leigh and Meredith - thank you for your endless support. Thank you for your late night and early morning texts and listening ears and words of encouragement.

To Wayne - thank you for your support during my illness.

Very special thanks go to my Pastor, Bishop Dwayne C, Debnam and his wife Elder Carla Debnam for their prayers and support. I also want to thank my Morning Star Baptist Church /MSBC Ministries Family whose support has been invaluable.

Last, but not least, to Leslie, my editor and publisher - thank you for your belief in me, for your transparency, tireless support and patience. You helped me create this project from what was literally written thoughts on pieces of paper. Thank you for pushing me to bring those scrambled words to order and life in this book. Thank you for your belief for this to come to pass.

AND THEN YOU GO SHOPPING

BEHIND MY PINK RIBBON

On July 24, 2009, around 6:30 pm, I received the call that would immediately change my life. That was the day I was told that I had cancer.

My immediate reaction was one of numbness and shock. At the time I had a husband and 2 sons, one aged 8 and the other one 12. I thought back to friends I knew who lost parents at a young age. I wondered what would happen to my sons if I did not "make it" through this. What type of legacy would I be leaving for them should I pass? Had I created enough memories for them to remember me years down the road?

Although it was a lot to process, I did not have a lot of time to stay in this phase, therefore I had to move forward. The following days and weeks consisted of various tests and procedures that would determine the stage of this disease and the course of treatment. The course of treatment that was decided for me was to include 8 weeks of chemotherapy, a full course of radiation, and several surgeries.

Due to the size of my tumor, it was decided that I would have 4 rounds of chemotherapy to shrink the tumor, followed by a lumpectomy. The second set of 4 rounds of chemotherapy was to take place after the lumpectomy. As it turned out, the tissue that was biopsied with the lumpectomy, revealed DCIS. DCIS is the presence of abnormal cells inside a milk duct in the breast. This type of cancer is considered to be non-invasive, which means it has not spread out of the milk duct. Due to the fact that I already had an invasive cancer in the same breast, my treatment was for me to undergo a mastectomy.

I don't remember asking God why He allowed this to happen to me.

I remember when I shared the news with a friend of mine, she stated "Oh no! I was praying that it would not be cancer." I remember telling her that it wasn't so much that God did not answer her prayer, it was more that He had a path for me to take. It was all a part of His Divine Plan. I determined early on that if this was the path that God had chosen for me, then He would get the glory out of it. My job was to seek His direction through the course.

On this journey, I learned many lessons. For one thing, I learned what really matters in life. In many ways, my relationship with God was strengthened. Many times, we place our trust in things and not God. If truth be told, those things will not even matter or exist a year from now.

I HAD NO OTHER OPTION, but to totally surrender and place my trust in God. I HAD no other choice but to let Him direct my path through this journey.

I would have preferred to have gone through treatment without any bumps or hurdles and come out unblemished. Instead God had and continues to have a Plan for me. I HAD to learn to continue to trust Him to bring me through those bumps and hurdles. Although I had experienced a lot of hurt and disappointments in my past, I learned that it was time to let many things go. I had to move past all of it in order to heal.

During this time of focus I had to be totally dependent on God and His healing power. I had a crash course in faith and perseverance. Throughout this course, God showed me that He always provides. During all of this, God provided many angels who walked and cried with me along the way. I am eternally grateful to them. My role changed from being the nurturer to the one who needed nurturing. The one who could multitask with the best of them, was now thankful to get one thing accomplished in a day.

When I found that lump back in 2009, little did I know how much I would find myself. I have literally walked through the valley of the shadow of death and come through renewed. Behind my pink ribbon is a woman who is fearfully and wonderfully made (Psalm 139:14 NIV) and knows it.

CHAPTER 1

HOPE

Yes, my soul, find rest in God; my hope comes from Him.

Psalms 62:5

GOING SHOPPING

Have you ever gone shopping, but didn't really feel like it? Maybe you were in the middle of preparing that special meal only to discover you were missing a vital ingredient. Your heart and mind are focused on the dish. You have laid out your ingredients and gotten your prep bowls ready, only to discover in the midst of it all that you are missing something. Instead of cooking, you have to interrupt everything to run to the store to purchase that missing ingredient. Or, maybe a friend called you to hang out with them at the mall when you only wanted to stay home and just chill. This is a good friend, so you oblige your friend and go shopping with them.

My unwanted shopping trip started on a Friday evening back in 2009 with six words, "I'm so sorry, you have cancer." Those six simple words would change my life forever. Little did I know how much. I accepted the diagnosis only from the standpoint of not denying that treatment was needed. I can't say however that I ever "owned" the diagnosis.

Yes, I knew that I was diagnosed with cancer. I accepted the diagnosis enough to accept treatment for it. I did not want that to define me or who I was. Although I did not want cancer to become a part of my identity, I also did not want to be blind to the fact that the cancer needed treatment. I believe in God's Healing. I also believe that God has placed persons here on earth to carry out His Directions for healing. My prayer was for God to place the correct persons in my treatment course. I asked that He provide them with the knowledge needed to define my treatment course. Included in this were all the persons that would be involved in all aspects of my care.

I also asked God to show me what He needed me to do through the journey I was about to take. One of my first thoughts was whether I would live to see my sons grow up. At the time, my oldest son was going into the eighth grade. Eighth grade was supposed to be the year of middle school graduation, high school visits and applications. What was going to happen to college goals and dreams? Our youngest son was going to the fourth grade. He was still a child with childhood innocence.

I felt as though the rug had been snatched from under me. I went through various stages of shock, disbelief, and anger. Although there is a history of cancer in my family, I was still shocked when the diagnosis was verbalized. I really could not believe I had received a cancer diagnosis. I had a history of biopsies, however they always turned out negative. Why did this time have to be any different? What happened?

I was angry because I followed all of the "rules" but still got cancer. Before the diagnosis, I had no real significant health problems. I did not have a smoking history. I rarely drank alcohol. I tried to maintain a relatively healthy lifestyle. This diagnosis seemed like another heartbreak on top of other heartbreaks that I had experienced. Why did it seem as though I was getting the heartbreaks? My emotions went back and forth between shock, disbelief and anger.

When I finally reached acceptance of the diagnosis, I went shopping. No, I did not go on a clothing or shoe shopping spree. Instead, I went shopping for inner resolve and inner strength. I searched for faith. The faith that only needed to be the size of a mustard seed, but could still move mountains. I searched for hope. My doctor said to me, "we will do everything to help you." Did he really mean what he was saying? Were these just words that are spoken to everybody when they are given a cancer diagnosis?

To an extent, what my doctor said was true. I could only hope they would do everything they could to help me. Immediately I spoke with God. The doctors would need guidance in terms of helping me. I asked God to provide the doctors that would have the knowledge and expertise for my treatment. I also asked God to guide and direct them as they looked through all the results from the imaging studies as my course of treatment would be discussed and determined.

I shopped some more. This time I filled my shopping basket with more prayers, more answers to questions, more information, more resources, more listening ears, and more support.

As people were told what was going on with me, I received additional prayers and promises of support. They shared their experiences of loved ones who had undergone cancer treatment. I was put in touch with several support groups from the very beginning. I found these support groups to be invaluable. They provided a wealth of information and understanding persons who had gone through what I was about to undergo. They understood the fears and thoughts I was experiencing.

As I shopped for peace, I asked God for the peace that Philippians 4:7 speaks of: "And the peace of God, which transcends all understanding, will guard your hearts and your minds in Christ Jesus." I needed the reassurance of peace that surpasses all understanding. Despite the unknown I was facing; I found comfort and hope in the scriptures.

I knew this was a shopping trip where there were no sales or discounts. Instead, it was head first, full speed ahead. There were no clearance items, no deals of the day, and no coupons. I could not take any shortcuts with my treatment. Everything had to be on point. I was literally in the fight of and for my life.

As I moved to acceptance, I remember God telling me that my illness was not to death. Instead, He had work for me to do. It was then that

I saw that I had to go through my journey to help others. Other persons needed to see and know that even with a cancer diagnosis, there is hope and one can still thrive.

FUN IN THE MIDST OF FEAR

"Anxiety weighs down the heart, but a kind word cheers it up"

Proverbs 12:25 NIV

After a whirlwind of testing, followed by test results and more doctors' appointments, I received what was to be my treatment plan. Throughout the testing process, every part of my body had been probed, poked at, and scanned. Eventually another body part was going to be surrendered for examination and eventually disposed of. My plan consisted of several surgeries, chemotherapy and radiation. Since my tumor was a rather sizable one, the treatment plan was for me to undergo chemotherapy to reduce its size prior to surgery.

I knew individuals who had undergone chemotherapy in the past, so I was well aware of its side effects. I also knew much had been done to ease those side effects of treatment. As weird as it may sound, I was not that concerned about losing all my hair. I figured that was the least of my worries.

One of the recommendations that is given in resource literature is to shop for a wig before you need it. I remember feeling angry because I was going to "have" to wear a wig. I had worn hair pieces in the past, however, in my mind, this was different because I "had to" wear a wig. I interpreted this as a loss of control over another part of my body. I did not want a "hair prosthesis," the medical term for wig that was used on the prescription the doctor wrote for me. Things may have changed, but at the time, it seemed as though those wigs screamed out "cancer wig." I decided that I would buy my own wig from a wig shop. I felt those wigs had a more natural look to them.

Late one evening, one of my cousins came down from Pennsylvania and took me wig shopping. Unbeknownst to me, she had already alerted the shop owner of my circumstances and my needs.

For those few hours, we did more than wig shop. We had a ball. The shop owner showed me wig after wig after wig. He brought out some ridiculous ones, which made me laugh. There were others that he combed into funny styles. The more

I laughed, the zanier he became.

I had many styles to choose from: short, long, curly, straight. I eventually settled on a short blunt cut with blond streaks in a style similar to the hairstyle I had at the time. For those few short hours, I was given the opportunity to have fun, despite the road ahead of me. Even though things were serious, I learned how to let things go, even if it was for just a few moments.

After my second chemotherapy treatment, my hair started to come out one evening as I was combing it. My eyelashes and eyebrows came out when I washed my face. Once I lost the hair on my head, I did not count on my head feeling like it was in a perpetual state of cold. Since I received chemotherapy during the winter months, the wig was more for warmth purposes than for vanity. As time went on and I eventually learned to accept wearing the wig, I always thought back to the fun I had that night in the wig store.

CHAPTER 2

TRUST

"For I know the plans I have for you," declares the Lord, "plans to prosper you and not to harm you, plans to give you hope and a future."

Jeremiah 29:11 NIV

WHAT AN ASSIGNMENT!

In some respects, I find the word chemotherapy an oxymoron. The Merriam-Webster Dictionary provides the following definition for chemotherapy: "the therapeutic use of chemical agents to treat disease." When we think of therapy, we usually think of something that helps us. However, with my course of chemotherapy, every 2 weeks my body was going to be assaulted with a chemical mixture that had all types of side effects, major and minor, both real and potential. On the other hand, this chemical mixture was needed to treat my cancer.

Chemotherapy has its own mind, its own course of action, and its own specific journey. Each round does not get easier. In fact, you are told that chemotherapy has a cumulative effect. I was apprehensive to say the least.

BUT I heard my God say "I still have work for you to do."

What came to my mind was Jesus praying in the Garden of Gethsemane. *Matthew 26:39 NIV "My Father, if it is possible, may this cup be taken from me. Yet not as I will, but as you will."*

I would not have raised my hand for this assignment. Between the uncertainty of the treatment outcome and the side effects of the treatment, the road ahead was going to be a rough one. I had to trust in God's Word and what He spoke to me. God told me that He still had work for me to do, so I had to believe that I would be an overcomer and come through in the end. I had to trust God to provide the doctors with the right treatment plan. Even though the treatment plan would leave me not feeling my best, I still had to trust the plan and the process for a favorable outcome.

I BOUGHT A SMILE

"So do not fear, for I am with you; do not be dismayed, for I am your God. I will strengthen you and help you; I will uphold you with my righteous right hand."

Isaiah 41:10 NIV

Next came the actual chemotherapy phase. So many thoughts raced through my mind. How would I feel? How would my body react to the drugs that were going to invade it? How much disruption would this mean for my day to day activities? How would I look? Would other people be able to tell that I had cancer just by looking at me?

On paper, it looked like I was "ready" to start treatment. My to do list was all checked off:

✔ Strong network of praying and caring people

✔ Meal preparation during treatment

✔ Child care

✔ Transportation

✔ Treatment room tour

✔ Work arrangements

✔ Emergency Plan

✔ Wig (aka head prosthesis)

Yes, to my knowledge, my checklist was completed. One thing that I was missing was a smile. It's usually not hard for me to engage in a smile. I often say that it is so much easier to smile, than it is to frown. Following my diagnosis though, I found my smile a little harder to come by. It's easy to say "don't worry" or "everything will be alright." When faced with a life challenging situation, it's not quite that easy to say or to think.

I was often reminded of the father in Mark 9 who brought his son who was possessed by a deaf and mute spirit to Jesus for healing. When the boy was overtaken by the spirit, the spirit would throw him to the ground in what was described as a seizure-like activity. In verse 23, Jesus tells the father that "everything is possible for one who believes." After being told that, the father exclaimed "I do believe; help me overcome my unbelief!" Much like that father, yes, I believed that I could be healed. My question though was if I would be healed.

The first day of the chemotherapy leg of my journey had arrived. My mind started racing with so many thoughts.

How will it feel? I heard so much about chemotherapy, but never heard anyone speak about how the medication actually felt. Although I had a port implanted in my chest for the administration of the medication, I still wondered whether or not the medicine would hurt.

Will I get sicker? I knew there were side effects. I wondered how debilitating the side effects would be. I wondered whether or not I would be able to function. It was important to me that I did not look sick to those on the outside. I did not want to look like what I was going through.

Will I get the right amount? I realized that I had to trust God to direct those persons who were responsible for mixing my medications. Although the doctors prescribed the formula, I prayed for God to guide and direct the pharmacy staff to interpret the prescription and apply it correctly for my benefit.

Will it work? This is where I had to place my greatest trust in God. I had to trust the Plan that He had provided to the doctors, nurses, and other staff persons. He told me that my sickness was not to death. I had to trust that everything was going to still work out for my good.

So much was going on in the world that I called my mind. My thoughts though seemed like just tiny spots in my world. The more that my mind raced, the more I needed a smile. A smile that was without words but said "Trust me, I got your back." A smile that said, "I'm putting on my fighting gloves with you."

As I sat in the big comfy chair receiving my treatment, my Heavenly Father reminded me that I was one of His children. He reminded me of His Promise to never leave me. He also reminded me of His Promise that I would survive and see my children grow up. I could feel His Arms surround me through His Presence. He reminded me that everything was going to be alright. Yes, at that moment I had a smile. The smile that came from deep within, despite the uncertainty of everything.

I PRAYED

"Trust In The Lord with all your heart, lean not to your own understanding. In all your ways acknowledge Him and He will make your paths straight".

Proverbs 3:6-7 NIV

The first day of chemotherapy was a blur of information, signatures, consent forms, and staff introductions. As I sat in the nice big comfy chair and as the medicine infused into my body, I prayed for the strength to get through the treatment. As I watched the activity around me, I prayed for all the health care professionals and volunteers who were working, not just with me, but with all the patients. I prayed for the medical and pharmacy staff who worked to determine the formulas and mixed the medications.

As I listened to all of my new instructions, I prayed for understanding of what I needed to do. I prayed that I got it all right and would be able to carry them out as directed.

As I looked at the others in the room with me, I prayed for all the others who were undergoing chemotherapy. I prayed that they would find peace, comfort, and strength as they went through their process.

As I sat attached to this tube that was supposed to contain the magic healing formula, I prayed and trusted that everything would be okay. Instead of focusing on my situation, I took the mindset that God was using me in this situation to pray for others who were going through a cancer journey. I became grateful for the opportunity to pray instead of wallowing in or getting stuck at "why me?" As I progressed through the 8 rounds of chemotherapy, I developed a deeper trust with God. There was nothing and no one else that I could rely on except God. I could not afford to even attempt to rely on my own abilities. As my body experienced various side effects, I could not trust my body in terms of how it would react at any given time. It was a trust that required my total surrender to God.

CHAPTER 3

FAITH

"Now faith is what we hope for and assurance about what we do not see."

Hebrews 11:1 (NIV)

We all like to think that we have faith. Many times, we proudly make the proclamation that we are keeping the faith. I've discovered that it's relatively easy to say that we have faith when things are going relatively well for us. It's even easier when we look out and can see what's in front of us.

What happens to that same faith when we are faced with a life changing experience in literally a matter of seconds? What happens when we are given a diagnosis of cancer or for that matter, any type of bad news? A cancer diagnosis in particular opens up such a large window of uncertainty. How do we put our faith into action in those circumstances? We pray, but do we really believe what we are praying? What do we draw from to have a prayer of faith? I found that God will provide opportunities where He will remind us of our past experiences. He will also use unsuspecting moments to reveal a Promise to us.

About 3 months into my initial treatment, it came time for my oldest son to take a placement test for a high school he was interested in attending. As I watched the various students file into the auditorium, I listened to their voices which were eager with anticipation of their next journey. Their thoughts were on their next four years of high school. My thoughts were on whether or not I was even going to survive the next few months. Although it may have been selfish, I wanted to see my sons grown and independent. I remember sitting in the school auditorium that morning and asking God if I was going to live so that I would have that opportunity. This is a time that I thought back to that father in Mark 9. Again, I believed, but I needed help for my unbelief.

Just as clear as I asked the question, God spoke to me and told me that not only would I live to see my son graduate from middle school, I would also live to see both he and his brother graduate high school and become independent young men. That Promise became the stimulus for my faith activation.

As I journeyed through my treatment regimen, I kept God's Promise from that Saturday morning foremost in my mind. In the meantime, I had to take things one day at a time. My treatment cycle consisted of doctor's appointments, lab work, medication before my treatment, the actual treatment followed by side effects and more medication. This cycle was repeated every other week. By the time I recovered from the treatment's side effects, it was time for the cycle to start all over again.

Through all of this, I had to look past my current situation of discomfort. I had to believe that although I could not see what was in front of me, God promised me that I would survive. Even though it got to the point where I dreaded the treatment cycle, I had to keep in my remembrance how God brought me through other challenging seasons in my life. No matter how I felt, I held fast to His Promise that indeed I would survive this.

The side effects by themselves were a lot to handle. The external side effects were obvious. The most obvious was the hair loss. I also experienced hyperpigmentation. My hands, feet, tips of my ears, fingers, toes, nail beds, and tongue all turned black. Most of the time I experienced what I can only describe as a "full" feeling in my stomach. I had an appetite; however, I did not have to eat a lot in order to feel full. There were medications that helped to alleviate many of the physical symptoms. Some of the side effects remain even to this day, they never went away.

My chemotherapy medication changed with my last 4 cycles. Although the side effects were not as grueling as the first 4 chemotherapy cycles, I experienced intense itching. This was not the kind of itching that one normally experiences with a mosquito bite. This kind of itching felt as though it was taking place at the bone. It seemed as though it was triggered by any type of movement. There was no way to scratch this itch. I was told to take an antihistamine to alleviate the itching. The problem with that was the antihistamine made me sleepy. I was still working and driving.

I ended up having to plan out when I would take the medication. Most of the time I took a dose once I got to work. Then it would be worn off by the time I left work. After coming home, I would take ½ the dose before I ate dinner. After dinner, I would get into the bed, take the other ½ of the dose, and attempt to stay as still as possible before I drifted off to sleep.

I was told that chemotherapy makes you feel as though you have the flu. I have never had the flu so I did not have a reference point. All I can say is that the common side effect I experienced throughout receiving chemotherapy was extreme fatigue. Although the radiation side effects were not as brutal, I experienced skin irritation and burning where the radiation was directed. Many times, I felt so horrible, it was hard to believe that I would survive the side effects, much less the actual cancer diagnosis.

After the initial chemotherapy and radiation, I was placed on an oral medication that I had to take daily for the next 5 years. (At my last visit my oncologist told me the guidelines have since changed to 10 years.) That medication produced another side effect. The primary side effect that I experienced was continuous joint pain. Some days were worse than others. On those days, I would just say to my family, "this is a slow day." That simply meant that it was going to take me a little longer to either move around or get something accomplished. Please understand I'm not mentioning the side effects to scare anyone out of treatment. What I'm speaking about was my experience. Each person's experience is different and unique to that individual. I have heard of persons running a 5K during their treatment. Like so many others who have been on this journey, I am a living testimony that despite the brutal effects of the treatment, one can still survive the treatment. No matter what your individual experience may be, you will make it through.

One of my favorite scriptures is the 121st Psalm. The King James Version of the scripture states "I will lift up mine eyes unto the hills from whence cometh my help. My help cometh from the Lord which made heaven and earth." This scripture has always given me comfort and reassurance. It reminds me that no matter what may be going on in my life, all I need to do is reach out to God for any help that I may need.

Around the time of my diagnosis, Fred Hammond released the single "They That Wait." When I heard the song for the first time on the radio, I took it as a sign that the song was released just for me. In the beginning of the song Fred Hammond states "for those of you that are going through, for those of us that are waiting on His Promise, understand God has not forgotten you. When times get tough you got to look up to Heaven and encourage yourself." Literally, the day the CD was released, I bought a copy. I played "They That Wait" tirelessly. Every time I went anywhere in my car, I played it. I played it on the way to doctor's appointments, radiation therapy, you name it. To this day, I still have no idea what other songs are on the CD because that is the only song I played.

Although there is always the fear of the unknown in any situation, I experienced firsthand that faith will always win over that fear. God had already provided me with His Promise. I had to reach back to that Promise despite how I felt. I had to have faith in the Process. If I believed in God's Promise, then I had to believe the Process.

As time went on, the manifestation of God's Promise to me took the shape of many forms. Although I had a fairly large tumor, it responded readily to the 8 rounds of chemotherapy. Chemotherapy was a rough, but a necessary part of my treatment. My surgery was considered a success in terms of tumor removal. With all praise and thanks to God, there was no indication of metastasis or spread of the cancer cells to other organs in my body. Although the chemotherapy took its toll on my body in terms of physical changes and total depletion of my physical strength, I did not experience everything that could have happened; in particular the more serious side effects of kidney, lung, or heart damage.

Some 5 years later, my son's high school graduation took place on a Sunday. By then, in addition to the chemotherapy and radiation, I had experienced 2 major surgeries. Before going to the graduation ceremony, I attended our early church service. The full circle moment came when our male choir sang a rendition of Fred Hammond's song "They That Wait" that morning. Who would have thought? The song was released in 2009. This was 5 years later!!!! Of all the song selections for THAT morning!!!

As far as I was concerned, that was no coincidence. It was God's confirmation of His fulfillment of the Promise that He made to me back on that Saturday morning when my son took his high school entrance exam. I was alive, cancer-free and recovered.

CHAPTER 4

PERSEVERANCE

"Let perseverance finish its work so that you may be mature and complete, not lacking anything".
James 1:4

PRESSING THROUGH

When we first moved into our home, one of my dreams was to plant a flower garden. Armed with my newly purchased garden tools, as I started digging, my neighbor at the time came over and very smugly informed me that our soil consisted of clay. He told me that nothing could ever grow there. I remember telling him that I could not accept that and that I was going to plant my flowers and they would grow. He shrugged his shoulders, gave me a smile and walked back into his house.

When we are faced with obstacles, do we give up or do we press through the obstacle whatever it may be? Do we settle in a pity party? Do we stay stuck in our obstacle?

The Merriam-Webster Dictionary defines perseverance as: "continued effort to do or achieve something despite difficulties, failure, or opposition." In my case, many of my difficulties were related to the many side effects I experienced as a result of my treatment. The surgeries left my body feeling physically assaulted. The chemotherapy and radiation left me completely drained of energy. It was the kind of fatigue and exhaustion that simply going to sleep could not help. Some of the medications that were prescribed following chemotherapy produced their own set of side effects. Despite all of this, I had to press on through the Process.

Just as new topsoil had to be provided in order to create a "new soil" for those flowers that I planted to grow and thrive, I had to look to and trust God to provide what I needed to keep moving forward despite what my present situation looked like. I remember a good friend of mine, who had recently completed cancer treatment prior to my diagnosis, told me "you can have a pity party, but you can't stay there." There were many days that I didn't feel like getting out of bed, much less carry on any type of day to day activities.

I learned perseverance throughout this process. I felt as though I had not only been hit by a tractor trailer, but that the tractor trailer had backed up and run me over again. There were many days that I just did not have the energy to move forward. Those were the days that I had to reach deep within and remember that my God would provide the energy, strength, and endurance I needed to push forward. I reflected on scriptures, often meditating on the 121st

Psalm. That scripture reminded me that God would supply all of my help. He would give me the energy I needed.

When all was said and done, just as the new topsoil became a part of the new foundation for my flower bed, the cancer diagnosis and treatment became the new foundation for a transformed me. The chemotherapy eliminated the cancer cells and, in their place, new cancer free cells were formed.

CHAPTER 5

COURAGE

"So do not fear, for I am with you; do not be dismayed, for I am your God. I will strengthen you and help you; I will uphold you with my righteous right hand".

Isaiah 41:10

RIGHT HERE ALL THE TIME

I have an older model car. The car has an outlet that was described to me as having the ability to broadcast music over the car radio system. At that time, you could hook your MP3 player into the outlet and it would play your music.

I tried the feature once when I first got my car. I plugged my MP3 player in, tapped the FM/AUX button, but to my dismay, it did not work. For years and years that port went unused.

Fast forward many years later. I was in a local discount store and ran into an acquaintance. She was purchasing a small cable cord that she said she was going to plug into her car's MP3 port with the other end of the cord going into her phone. She said she used that as a Bluetooth.

I purchased a cord and once again tried to hook my phone to the MP3 port in my car, thinking it could be a great alternative the next time I either forgot my Bluetooth or misplaced it. I ripped open the package and plugged one end into the port. The other end I plugged into my phone. Very eagerly, I tapped the FM/AUX button on my dashboard, only to discover that once again, this feature did not work. I said "oh well" and placed the cable into my car console.

Fast forward a few more months.

Our family was taking a short car trip to return our son back to his base. Like I'm sure similar to a lot of families, there are several car trip rules. First and foremost, if I'm driving, there has to be music. For me, the music has to be upbeat. If anyone goes to sleep, I sing.

My son volunteered to play the music that he had loaded on his phone. I casually mentioned the cable I bought that was supposed to link up with my car's stereo system didn't work.

My son very simply took the cable, attached it to his phone, and then plugged it into the port on the dashboard. From there he tapped the switch that indicated FM/AUX. This time he tapped the switch twice. Immediately we were provided with music coming through the car's sound system. The ability to work the FM/AUX button was there all the time. It just needed the proper activation in order to work. Even though it appeared that way, the AUX feature was not broken. Everything that I needed to work the AUX feature was right at my fingertips all the time.

Similarly, I needed to activate my courage. I needed courage to face the cancer journey. Courage as I waited for testing results that would determine the stage of cancer I was diagnosed with. Courage through multiple surgeries. Courage through treatment and treatment side effects. Courage to face the unknown future. Although none of us know what lies ahead of us minute to minute, God has already promised us that He is with us all the time. God had already supplied me with the courage I needed. All I needed to do was tap into the resources that God had for me in order to activate that courage. Tapping into courage allowed me to handle not only the treatment, but the fear of the unknown. I needed courage to keep me from becoming paralyzed with fear.

Becoming paralyzed with fear would result in my inability to move forward as a result of being overwhelmed in the what ifs. What if the treatment did not work? What if the treatment produced permanent side effects? What if I got the wrong amount of medicine? What if I had the wrong treatment plan for the type of cancer that I had?

Just like my son simply tapped the AUX control the correct way, all I needed to do was tap into God at each step of my journey for courage. With all of the instructions that came flying at me that I needed to process, it was very easy to get overwhelmed and feel defeated. I found it worked better for me to break things down step by step, asking God for courage at each step.

CHAPTER 6

PEACE

"Cast Your Cares On The Lord and He Will Sustain You"

Psalm 55:22 (NIV)

IMAGINE THOSE THINGS THAT ARE NOT

Each treatment produced its own set of side effects. For the first four rounds of chemotherapy, the side effects I experienced were similar to flu symptoms. I experienced hot and cold sweats, bone and body aches, and extreme fatigue with each treatment. Each treatment was cumulative which meant that the symptoms would increase with each round. I knew that in order to get to the healing process I had to go through the treatment process. It got to the point where I actually dreaded each treatment. It wasn't so much the infusion. It was the side effects that I knew were coming that I dreaded. I experienced anticipatory anxiety, meaning I was anxious over expectations, not the actual experience. In order to help combat this feeling, I prayed for peace and calmness.

Using imagery helped me get through this process physically. I imagined the various side effects working in my favor. I imagined my body going through the healing process of release, regeneration, and restoration.

For instance, as the sweat poured from what felt like every pore in my body, I thought release. Release from the standpoint of letting go. In this case, I thought about the release of the

49

cancer cells that threatened to invade my body. In my mind, each drop of sweat represented the release of those cells from my body. The more I sweat, the more my body released those dangerous toxins.

As I ached, I imagined regeneration. Regeneration of fresh, new cells. In my mind, fresh new cells were at work replacing the old diseased ones. I thought about how plants need to be pruned in order for new shoots to come from the plant. When the supply to the unhealthy portion of the plant is cut off, a fresh, young shoot will appear along the same stem. As the chemotherapy destroyed whatever was fueling the old diseased cells, new cells were being grown and formed.

I likened the extreme fatigue I endured to restoration. Some of us like to restore old items for a new use. In order to do this, a lot of times the old item needs to be stripped of all its paint, varnish, and other finishing's in order to apply the new finish. In terms of my body, it was as though it was being stripped down to its very core.

Throughout all of this, I was reminded of just how much God really cared for me. Despite the fact that most days I felt as though I had been continuously beat upon, I could feel God's Presence in me. I was thankful that there were medications that I could take to alleviate the nausea I was experiencing. Yes, I felt worse than terrible most of the time, however that was the nature of what was needed to achieve a better outcome. The better outcome was that of cancer purging itself from my body. Substituting the awful side effects to thinking in the positive, gave me peace.

Oftentimes, I now think of the areas in life that need to be purged in order to have that closer, intimate relationship with God. Is it worry to the point of not being able to function? Or is it the worry that gets to the feeling of giving up? What is it that is hindering a stronger relationship with God? Are every day cares and activities shutting out God's Voice?

1 Peter 5:7 tells us to "cast our anxiety on Him because He cares for us." God is waiting for us to talk with Him and to tell Him how we feel. He already knows what we are in need of. He knows what we need to release. When we talk with Him, we show that we have trust in Him to work things out according to His Plan.

The King James version of Philippians 4:7 tells us "And the peace of God, which passeth all understanding, shall keep your hearts and minds through Christ Jesus." I found that the more that I trusted God, the more peaceful I felt. I found peace in knowing that God cared for me. Since God cared for me, I could feel safe trusting in Him.

GOD'S FINAL HEAL

"For I have fought the good fight, I have finished the race, I have kept the faith."

2 Timothy 4:7-8

In November of 2015, I attended a victory celebration for a friend who had been pronounced cancer free after her 3rd bout with the disease. Not long after the celebration, it was discovered that not only had the disease recurred, but this time the disease had spread to her bones. She told me that this time, the pain was much worse than before. She hung in there though, doing as much as she could to keep up with her day to day routine.

Then, what started as a trip to the doctor turned into her transition to what I call her final heal. She was admitted to the hospital and started on a treatment that would try to arrest cancer's final rampage through her body systems. Each time I visited her; I could see the effects that the disease had taken on her body. I felt selfish because I wanted her with me a little more time. We still had so many things that we talked about accomplishing together. Despite all that she was going through, she still remembered that I was preparing for ordination as a Deaconess. She even mentioned she was looking forward to getting discharged so that she could attend the ordination service.

My spiritual discernment however told me that this time, she was preparing for her final heal. As she started her transition, God started to prepare me as well. Although the selfish part of me would have loved for her to have stayed a little while longer on this earth, I took comfort in knowing that she would soon be in the Bosom of our Father. I realized that He would soon be rocking her in His arms. She would soon be relieved from all the pain that she had endured on earth. Although we will no longer be able to talk about our chemotherapy hairstyles, she would have her royal crown resting securely on her head.

So many times, I hear the phrase that a person has either won or lost their fight with cancer. My friend taught me that even though a person leaves us physically, they did not lose their battle or fight with cancer. I would like to think that they are the true winners. Isaiah 53:5 tells us "......and by His stripes we are healed." My friend, like so many others, fought her good fight here on earth. Her body, which was formerly ravaged by cancer, was now transformed through God's final heal, to her heavenly body. Her body was now without spot, blemish, or pain. Although I said goodbye to her on this earth, my comfort and peace is in knowing that I will see her again in her heavenly home.

CHAPTER 7

THE JOURNEY MOVES FORWARD

"For I know the plans I have for you," declares the Lord, "plans to prosper you and not to harm you, plans to give you hope and a future.

Jeremiah 29:11 NIV

THE NEW ME

Praise God!!!

I have been cancer-free for 10 years. These years have been filled with highs and lows. Although I would not have volunteered for this journey, I have learned so much during this time.

During my toughest days on this journey, I learned about the ministry of presence. I had friends who stopped by just to sit with me. Although there were times that I was too weak to offer much conversation, they were content to just be there with me.

I learned what a true village is. My village consisted of a community of persons who prayed, provided listening ears, cooked meals, cleaned, baby sat, provided rides to appointments and treatments, provided rides to work, gave encouragement, visited, and the list goes on. On the list is pretty much anything that helped to provide comfort and help make a difficult situation so much better. I am truly blessed and appreciative of my village.

I dare not start to list names. Just know that you are deeply appreciated for all that you ever did for me. No act of kindness was too small, nor did it go unnoticed. Words cannot express my gratitude for the acts of kindness. I'm grateful for my village that still exists even 10 years later.

I learned not to sweat the small things that we can get caught up in. When one comes out of a true life or death situation, one learns very quickly what's really important. What's important is discovering and walking in God's Purpose for your life. Even in times of adversity, which does not necessarily entail a cancer diagnosis, we can look to God and seek His Plan for our lives.

It was important for me to learn the lessons that God wanted me to experience through my cancer journey. First and foremost, I learned that I am stronger than I ever thought I could be. My walk with God became even stronger as I learned to trust Him and His Plans. Having faith in His Promise gave me the courage and strength to persevere through the surgeries, treatments, additional scares, and recuperation periods. Trusting Him gives me an inner peace which can only come from recognizing that His Presence is always with me.

I currently serve on our church's cancer support ministry. Members of our ministry partner with persons who reach out to the ministry for assistance and support. We serve to guide persons through their treatment and beyond.

My sons are now young adults. One son has completed his military service. The other son is a college student. Many times, I feel as though they had to grow up faster than others. Because I was physically unable to do household activities most of the time, they learned how to do many things as children that many do not learn until they are much older. They were given crash courses on how to take care of their clothes and how to cook basic meals. One time I tried to fix Easter dinner only to have to lay back down due to exhaustion. I remember laying down on the sofa and giving my oldest son directions on how to finish what I had started.

Before my diagnosis I always felt as though I appreciated life. This journey has taken that appreciation to a totally different level. The simple act of waking up and climbing out of bed in the morning is not taken for granted. I remember my Pastor preaching a sermon "What Really Matters" shortly after I was diagnosed. Surviving cancer and going through the survivor process has taught me a greater appreciation for people. I am grateful for those opportunities to serve and to be of service to others.

There will always be challenges. Persevering through this cancer journey has strengthened my trust, faith, hope, and courage. My trust in God through the Process, whatever the Process may be for the situation. I learned how to activate my faith and how to maintain my faith in spite of what current circumstances may appear. My hope is for a better future. I have greater courage. The courage to stay strong when circumstances say otherwise. After shopping for and receiving trust, faith, hope, courage, and perseverance, I have peace in knowing that all things will work together according to God's Favor in my life.

ABOUT THE AUTHOR

Karen is originally from Queens, New York. She is currently a resident of Maryland. Her goal is to inspire others and let them know that although life may deal a blow that literally takes your breath away, exercising your faith and trust in God will give you the victory to prevail. She believes that life is a journey of experiences that can only be mastered with God's help and guidance.

If you would like to book Karen for speaking engagements of encouragement, please email her at authorkjay@gmail.com.